The Mayans
A Quick Read

The Mayans

Mayan Civiliz

The Maya civilization, renowned for its achievements in science, mathematics flourished in Mesoamerica for over tw Spanning a vast region that includes Guatemala, Belize, Honduras, and El Salvador, the Maya left an indelible mark on history through their remarkable cultural and intellectual contributions.

At the heart of the Maya civilization was a complex social and political structure. City-states formed the backbone of Maya society, each governed by a divine ruler known as a "k'uhul ajaw." These rulers, considered intermediaries between the earthly and divine realms, held tremendous power and were responsible for maintaining order and overseeing the religious rituals and ceremonies that played a central role in Maya life.

One of the most extraordinary aspects of Maya civilization was its advancements in science and mathematics. The Maya developed a sophisticated system of mathematics, using a base-20 numeral system and the concept of zero, centuries before it was recognized in other parts of the world. This mathematical prowess allowed them to make precise astronomical observations and create accurate calendars that tracked celestial events with remarkable precision.

The Maya writing system, known as hieroglyphs, was another remarkable achievement. The Maya scribes meticulously recorded their history, myths, rituals, and scientific knowledge on stone monuments, stucco walls, and codices made of bark paper. Although the decipherment of Maya hieroglyphs is an ongoing endeavor, significant progress has been made in understanding this intricate script, revealing insights into Maya history, religion, and culture.

Art was a vibrant expression of Maya civilization. Maya artists created breathtaking sculptures, intricate pottery, and vivid murals that depicted scenes from everyday life, religious

3

ceremonies, and mythological narratives. These artistic masterpieces not only showcased the Maya's technical skill but also provided a window into their cosmology, worldview, and social hierarchy.

Religion played a central role in Maya society, permeating all aspects of life. The Maya worshipped a pantheon of gods and goddesses who governed natural forces and human affairs. Elaborate ceremonies, rituals, and sacrifices were conducted to ensure the well-being of the community and maintain the delicate balance between the earthly and supernatural realms.

Despite the decline of the ancient Maya civilization around the 10th century CE, the legacy of their achievements endures. Archaeologists and scholars continue to uncover new insights into the Maya's extraordinary achievements and unravel the mysteries of their culture. Today, Maya ruins such as Tikal, Palenque, and Chichen Itza draw visitors from around the world, providing glimpses into the architectural marvels and cultural depth of this remarkable civilization.

In conclusion, the Maya civilization stands as a testament to human ingenuity and cultural brilliance. Their advancements in science, mathematics, writing, and art place them among the great civilizations of the ancient world. The Maya's profound understanding of the natural and supernatural realms, their complex social structure, and their artistic achievements continue to inspire awe and admiration, reminding us of the rich tapestry of human history and the enduring legacy of the Maya civilization.

Geography of the Mayan

The Maya Civilization, which thrived in Mesoamerica from approximately 2000 BCE to 1500 CE, was a remarkable ancient civilization known for its advanced knowledge in various fields, including mathematics, astronomy, and architecture. The geographical environment in which the Maya lived played a significant role in shaping their civilization and way of life.

The Maya civilization was predominantly located in the region that encompasses modern-day Mexico, Belize, Guatemala, Honduras, and El Salvador. This area is characterized by diverse landscapes, ranging from dense rainforests to limestone plateaus and coastal plains. The Maya adapted to these varied environments and developed distinct settlements based on their geographical features.

The dense rainforests of the Maya lowlands provided fertile soil for agriculture, which formed the backbone of the Maya civilization. The Maya developed sophisticated farming techniques, including slash-and-burn agriculture and terraced farming, to cultivate crops such as maize, beans, and squash. The availability of fertile land allowed for the establishment of large-scale agricultural settlements and supported a dense population.

In addition to agriculture, the Maya utilized the abundant natural resources found in their surroundings. They exploited the forests for timber, constructing impressive structures using large stone blocks and carving intricate sculptures. The Maya also utilized rivers and cenotes, natural sinkholes with freshwater, for transportation, irrigation, and as a source of drinking water.

The diverse geography of the Maya region led to the development of distinct city-states with unique characteristics. The northern Yucatan Peninsula, for example, featured a limestone plateau with few natural water sources. To overcome this challenge, the Maya constructed underground cisterns called chultuns to collect rainwater. Chichen Itza and Tulum are well-known cities that emerged in this region.

The southern Maya lowlands, on the other hand, were characterized by extensive river systems such as the Usumacinta and the Grijalva. These rivers provided both transportation and fertile land for agriculture. Cities like Palenque and Tikal flourished in this region, showcasing magnificent architectural achievements, including towering temples and intricate palaces.

The coastal regions offered access to marine resources and facilitated trade and communication with other civilizations through maritime routes. The city of Tulum, situated on the east coast of the Yucatan Peninsula, served as a prominent port and trading hub for the Maya.

The geographical diversity of the Maya region also influenced the religious and cultural beliefs of the civilization. The Maya revered natural elements such as caves, cenotes, and mountains, considering them sacred and closely associated with their deities. The distinct landscapes served as backdrops for religious rituals and ceremonies.

In conclusion, the geography of the Maya region played a crucial role in shaping the civilization's development. The fertile rainforests, river systems, coastal plains, and limestone plateaus provided resources, agricultural opportunities, and facilitated trade and communication. The Maya's ability to adapt to and harness the geographical features of their surroundings contributed to the creation of one of the most remarkable ancient civilizations in history.

Mayan City-States

In the heart of ancient Mesoamerica, the Mayan civilization flourished with a unique and sophisticated urban landscape characterized by city-states. These city-states were the focal points of Mayan society, serving as political, economic, and cultural hubs that thrived amidst the dense jungles of present-day Mexico, Guatemala, Belize, Honduras, and El Salvador.

At the core of Mayan city-states lay a complex social and political structure. Each city-state was governed by a divine king who held both political and religious authority. The ruler, often considered a divine intermediary between the people and the gods, wielded significant power over their subjects. Beneath the ruler were nobles and elites who aided in governance and administration, while the common people engaged in various trades, agriculture, and crafts.

Mayan city-states were characterized by their monumental architecture, including towering pyramids, sprawling palaces, and intricate ball courts. These impressive structures served not only as symbols of power and prestige but also as centers for religious ceremonies, political gatherings, and community events. The Mayans were master builders, utilizing advanced techniques in construction and engineering to create awe-inspiring edifices that still captivate the imagination today.

Trade played a crucial role in the prosperity of Mayan city-states. Despite the dense rainforests that surrounded them, the Mayans developed extensive trade networks that connected distant regions. Goods such as jade, obsidian, cacao, and feathers flowed between city-states, facilitating both economic exchange and cultural diffusion. These trade routes not only enriched the city-states economically but also fostered cultural exchange and interaction among diverse communities.

Religion permeated every aspect of Mayan life, and city-states were no exception. Temples dedicated to various gods dotted the urban landscape, where priests conducted elaborate rituals and ceremonies to appease the deities and ensure the well-being of the community. The Mayans believed in a complex pantheon of gods and goddesses associated with natural elements, celestial bodies, and societal roles, reflecting their deep reverence for the natural world and their place within it.

Despite their shared cultural heritage, Mayan city-states were not always unified. Instead, they often engaged in conflicts and alliances, vying for power and resources in a competitive geopolitical landscape. Warfare was a common feature of Mayan society, with city-states frequently clashing over territory, tribute, and political dominance. However, warfare was also ritualized, with captives often being used for religious sacrifices rather than annihilation.

The decline of the Mayan city-states remains a subject of debate among scholars, with various factors contributing to their eventual collapse. Environmental degradation, population pressures, political instability, and internal strife are among the proposed explanations for the decline of Mayan urban centers. By the end of the 9th century AD, many of the once-great city-states lay abandoned, reclaimed by the encroaching jungle, leaving behind enigmatic ruins that continue to intrigue and inspire awe.

In conclusion, Mayan city-states were vibrant centers of civilization that flourished amidst the jungles of ancient Mesoamerica. Characterized by complex social hierarchies, monumental architecture, extensive trade networks, and rich religious traditions, these urban centers were the beating heart of Mayan society. Despite their eventual decline, the legacy of the Mayan city-states endures as a testament to the ingenuity, creativity, and resilience of one of the world's great civilizations.

Chichen Itza

Chichen Itza, a magnificent archaeological site located in the Yucatan Peninsula of Mexico, stands as a testament to the rich history and remarkable achievements of the ancient Mayan civilization. This UNESCO World Heritage site offers visitors a captivating glimpse into the cultural and architectural brilliance of the Mayans.

Chichen Itza flourished between the 9th and 12th centuries CE, reaching its peak as a major regional center of the Mayan civilization. It served as a hub for political, economic, and religious activities, attracting thousands of inhabitants and visitors from neighboring regions. The site's significance lies in its fusion of Mayan and Toltec cultures, resulting in a unique architectural style that reflects both influences.

The most iconic structure within Chichen Itza is the towering pyramid known as El Castillo or the Temple of Kukulcan. This step-pyramid showcases precise astronomical alignments and intricate stone carvings. The Great Ball Court, the largest in Mesoamerica, reveals the Mayans' passion for the Mesoamerican ballgame. El Caracol, an astronomical observatory, stands as a testament to the Mayans' advanced understanding of celestial movements.

The Cenote of Sacrifice, a natural sinkhole within Chichen Itza, played a significant role in Mayan rituals. It was believed to be a sacred gateway to the underworld. Archeological discoveries have revealed various artifacts and human remains, suggesting that sacrifices, including valuable objects and individuals, were offered to appease the gods. Today, visitors can marvel at the cenote's natural beauty and ponder its historical significance.

Chichen Itza continues to captivate and inspire visitors with its awe-inspiring architecture, rich history, and cultural significance. It stands as a testament to the Mayans' exceptional knowledge in astronomy, engineering, and artistic expression. As one of the New Seven Wonders of the World, Chichen Itza serves as a reminder of the extraordinary achievements of ancient civilizations and the importance of preserving our collective human heritage for future generations.

El Castillo

El Castillo, or "The Castle," is one of the most iconic and impressive structures found at the ancient Mayan city of Chichen Itza, located in the Yucatan Peninsula of Mexico. This magnificent pyramid stands as a testament to the architectural and astronomical prowess of the Mayan civilization, captivating visitors with its grandeur and significance.

Rising approximately 30 meters (98 feet) high, El Castillo dominates the surrounding landscape, serving as a focal point for the city and a symbol of Mayan power and authority. Constructed during the Terminal Classic period (c. 800-1000 AD) and modified in subsequent centuries, El Castillo represents a culmination of Mayan architectural achievements, blending both religious and astronomical symbolism in its design.

The pyramid consists of nine terraced levels, each representing a different cosmic realm according to Mayan cosmology. A central stairway leads to the temple located at the summit, where rituals and ceremonies were conducted by Mayan priests. The four stairways on each side of the pyramid converge at the top, creating a total of 365 steps, symbolizing the solar year.

One of the most remarkable features of El Castillo is its alignment with the movements of the sun. During the spring and autumn equinoxes, a fascinating phenomenon occurs where the sun casts shadows on the pyramid, creating the illusion of a serpent descending along the stairway. This phenomenon is a testament to the Mayans' advanced understanding of astronomy and their ability to incorporate celestial events into their architecture and religious practices.

The temple chamber located at the summit of El Castillo is dedicated to Kukulkan, the feathered serpent deity associated with fertility, rain, and agricultural abundance. Carvings and sculptures of Kukulkan adorn the walls of the chamber, emphasizing the deity's importance in Mayan religious beliefs and rituals.

Beyond its religious significance, El Castillo also served as a marker for the passage of time and the cycles of the agricultural calendar. The orientation of the pyramid and its alignment with the movements of the sun allowed the Mayans to accurately determine important agricultural dates, such as the beginning of the planting and harvesting seasons.

Despite its imposing appearance and architectural sophistication, El Castillo also holds secrets waiting to be discovered. In recent years, researchers have utilized non-invasive techniques such as LiDAR (Light Detection and Ranging) to uncover hidden chambers and structures within the pyramid, suggesting that it may have served additional ceremonial or administrative functions beyond its outward appearance.

Today, El Castillo stands as a UNESCO World Heritage Site and a symbol of Mexico's rich cultural heritage. It continues to inspire awe and wonder in visitors from around the world, serving as a reminder of the ingenuity, creativity, and spiritual depth of the ancient Mayan civilization. Whether viewed from the ground or experienced firsthand by climbing its steps, El Castillo remains an enduring symbol of the enduring legacy of the Mayan people and their extraordinary achievements in architecture, astronomy, and culture.

Calakmul

Nestled in the heart of the Yucatán Peninsula, the ancient Mayan city of Calakmul emerges as a testament to the grandeur and historical significance of Mesoamerican civilization. Flourishing during the Classic period (250 CE to 900 CE), Calakmul was a powerhouse that played a pivotal role in shaping the political and cultural landscape of the Maya world.

Calakmul served as the primary seat of the Snake Kings, a lineage of powerful Maya rulers who left an enduring imprint on the city's history. The Snake Kings, associated with the title derived from serpent iconography, wielded significant political power at the pinnacle of their influence. This power extended beyond the confines of Calakmul, impacting the entire Maya region and contributing to the complexity of Mesoamerican politics.

At the heart of Calakmul's significance lies its longstanding rivalry with the equally influential city of Tikal, a rivalry known as the Tikal-Calakmul Wars. This protracted conflict spanned centuries and had profound implications for the political dynamics of the Maya region. Calakmul, under the leadership of the Snake Kings, played a central role in these wars, engaging in military campaigns and forging strategic alliances to assert its dominance.

The architectural prowess of Calakmul is evident in the grand structures commissioned by the Snake Kings. Towering pyramids, majestic palaces, and intricate stelae adorned the cityscape, showcasing the rulers' political authority and cultural sophistication. These structures were not merely monuments to power; they also served as platforms for elaborate ritualistic ceremonies that reinforced the divine connections of the Snake Kings, creating a tapestry of religious and political symbolism.

Calakmul's urban planning reflected a meticulous design, emphasizing both functionality and symbolism. The city boasted impressive causeways, plazas, and residential areas, highlighting its role as a political and administrative center. The Snake Kings' commitment to creating a monumental cityscape underscored their prestigious lineage and left an architectural legacy that influenced subsequent Mayan cities.

The hieroglyphic inscriptions found on stelae and monuments within Calakmul provide invaluable insights into the genealogy, achievements, and political strategies of the Snake Kings. The advanced Maya writing system, showcased in these inscriptions, allows modern scholars to unravel the complex history of Calakmul and its rulers, providing a window into the cultural and political dynamics of the Maya civilization.

Calakmul's influence extended beyond its own borders through strategic alliances and marriage connections forged by the Snake Kings. This network of power transcended individual city boundaries, contributing to the longevity of the Snake Kings' dynasty and solidifying their status as paramount rulers within the Maya region.

Despite its historical significance, Calakmul faced challenges and periods of decline, mirroring the cyclical nature of power and influence in Maya civilization. Environmental factors, warfare, and shifting alliances all played roles in the waxing and waning of Calakmul's dominance. The decline of the city marked the end of an era, but the legacy of Calakmul and the Snake Kings persisted in the annals of Maya history.

In conclusion, the Mayan city of Calakmul stands as a monumental symbol of the political, cultural, and architectural achievements of the ancient Maya civilization. Its significance, deeply intertwined with the legacy of the Snake Kings, reverberates through the centuries, leaving an indelible imprint on the landscape of Mesoamerican history.

El Mirador

El Mirador, nestled deep within the heart of the Petén jungle in northern Guatemala, stands as a testament to the grandeur of the ancient Maya civilization. This sprawling archaeological site, shrouded in lush greenery, holds the remnants of one of the largest and most influential cities of the pre-Columbian era. El Mirador's significance lies not only in its architectural marvels but also in its role as a political, economic, and cultural hub that shaped the trajectory of Mayan civilization.

The city of El Mirador flourished during the Preclassic period (2000 BCE to 250 CE), making it one of the earliest and most enduring centers of Maya culture. Its strategic location within the dense rainforest provided both challenges and advantages for its inhabitants. The architects of El Mirador ingeniously adapted to their environment, constructing massive structures that merged seamlessly with the natural landscape.

At the heart of El Mirador lies the monumental architectural complex known as La Danta, one of the largest pyramids of the ancient world. Rising 230 feet above the jungle floor, La Danta comprises several superimposed platforms and structures, showcasing the Mayans' advanced engineering and construction techniques. The significance of La Danta extends beyond its sheer size; it served as a symbolic representation of the city's power and authority.

The city's layout reflects a meticulous urban planning strategy. El Mirador featured an intricate network of causeways, plazas, and residential areas, emphasizing the city's role as a political and administrative center. The integration of elevated walkways and plazas allowed for efficient movement within the city while also facilitating social and ceremonial gatherings. El Mirador's urban design laid the foundation for subsequent Mayan cities, influencing the development of other major centers throughout Mesoamerica.

Beyond its architectural prowess, El Mirador played a pivotal role in the political dynamics of the ancient Maya. The city's rulers held significant influence over the surrounding region, establishing a complex political hierarchy. El Mirador's rulers engaged in political alliances, trade relationships, and conflicts with neighboring city-states, contributing to the intricate web of interregional interactions that characterized ancient Mesoamerica.

Economically, El Mirador thrived due to its strategic location and access to vital resources. The city controlled key trade routes and maintained a robust agricultural system, harnessing the fertile soils of the surrounding region. This economic prosperity fueled the construction of grand structures and supported a thriving population.

Culturally, El Mirador left an indelible mark on the Maya civilization. The city's religious and ceremonial centers, adorned with intricate stelae and altars, provided a backdrop for the worship of deities and the performance of elaborate rituals. El Mirador's cultural legacy extended to its artistic achievements, including finely crafted pottery, sculptures, and murals that showcased the Maya's sophisticated artistic sensibilities.

Despite its historical significance, El Mirador experienced a decline and eventual abandonment during the Late Preclassic period. The reasons behind the city's downfall remain a subject of scholarly debate, with factors such as environmental degradation, resource depletion, and political instability likely playing a role.

In conclusion, the Mayan city of El Mirador stands as a monumental testament to the ingenuity and cultural richness of the ancient Maya civilization.

Tikal

The ancient city of Tikal, nestled in the lush lowland rainforests of present-day Guatemala, stands as a testament to the grandeur and cultural sophistication of the Mayan civilization during the Classic period (250 CE to 900 CE). Tikal emerged as one of the most influential city-states in Mesoamerica, playing a pivotal role in shaping the political, architectural, and cultural landscape of the Maya world.

At the heart of Tikal's significance was its ambition for regional dominance. The city-state's strategic location in the lowlands allowed it to thrive in a diverse ecosystem, fostering agricultural productivity and sustaining a large population. Tikal's rulers, driven by a desire to assert their city's supremacy, engaged in a dynamic interplay of political maneuvering, military strategy, and architectural innovation.

Tikal's architectural prowess is exemplified by its iconic skyline dominated by towering limestone pyramids. These structures, such as the Temple of the Great Jaguar and the Temple of the Mask, served not only as monumental expressions of power but also as platforms for ritualistic ceremonies that reinforced the divine connections of Tikal's rulers. The cityscape featured expansive plazas, ball courts, and residential areas, showcasing a meticulous urban planning that emphasized both functionality and symbolic significance.

The rulers of Tikal, often associated with elaborate hieroglyphic inscriptions found on stelae and monuments, sought to immortalize their achievements and political strategies. The advanced Maya writing system allowed these inscriptions to provide invaluable insights into Tikal's genealogy, political alliances, and monumental events. The recorded history on these stone monuments served as a historical record, enabling modern scholars to unravel the complex narrative of Tikal's rise to prominence.

Tikal's influence extended beyond its architectural and political achievements. The city played a central role in the intricate web of Maya geopolitics, engaging in alliances and conflicts with neighboring city-states. The Tikal-Calakmul Wars, a protracted conflict spanning centuries, exemplified Tikal's ambition for regional dominance and its active participation in the complex political dynamics of the Maya region.

The economic prosperity of Tikal was closely tied to its agricultural practices, facilitated by sophisticated farming techniques that utilized the fertile lowland soils. Tikal's ability to sustain a large population contributed to its prominence as a political and cultural center. The city's trade networks facilitated the exchange of goods, further enhancing Tikal's significance in the broader Maya civilization.

Despite its periods of ascendancy, Tikal, like many ancient civilizations, experienced phases of decline. Factors such as environmental stress, resource depletion, and internal unrest played roles in the ebb and flow of Tikal's dominance. However, the legacy of Tikal persisted, influencing subsequent Mayan cities and contributing to the enduring cultural and historical tapestry of Mesoamerica.

In conclusion, Tikal stands as a monumental symbol of Mayan cultural and political achievements during the Classic period. Its grand architecture, intricate hieroglyphic inscriptions, and active participation in regional conflicts highlight the complexity and sophistication of Tikal's role in shaping the Maya world. The legacy of Tikal, preserved in its monumental structures and historical records, continues to captivate and inform our understanding of the rich history of the ancient Mayan civilization.

Mayan Government

The Maya civilization, known for its remarkable cultural achievements, also had a complex system of government that played a crucial role in their society. A closer look at Maya government provides valuable insights into their political organization, social structure, and decision-making processes.

The Maya civilization was not a unified empire but rather a collection of independent city-states. Each city-state had its own ruler, known as the ahau or king, who held political and religious authority. The ahau was believed to have divine lineage and acted as the intermediary between the gods and the people.

At the city-state level, government administration was hierarchical. The ruler was supported by a council of nobles and advisors, known as the ajawob. These nobles held significant positions of power and influence, and their roles included managing administrative affairs, overseeing the economy, and serving as military commanders.

Beneath the nobility were the common people, who were responsible for various duties such as farming, construction, and craftwork. While they did not have direct political power, they contributed to the functioning of society through their labor and participation in communal activities.

The Maya government had a decentralized structure, with each city-state operating independently. However, there were also instances of political alliances and conflicts between different city-states. These alliances were often formed through marriages between ruling families or through trade networks, creating a complex web of political relationships.

Decisions within the Maya government were made through a process of consultation and consensus-building. The ruler and the council of nobles would discuss important matters and seek input from advisors and respected members of the community. This collaborative approach allowed for a broad representation of perspectives and ensured the participation of different stakeholders.

Religion played a significant role in Maya government, as it was believed that the ruler had a sacred duty to maintain cosmic balance and appease the gods. Rituals, ceremonies, and sacrifices were conducted to seek divine guidance and blessings for the well-being of the city-state.

The Maya government also had a system of law and justice. Punishments for crimes varied depending on the severity of the offense and could range from fines to corporal punishment. The ruler and the nobles served as judges and arbiters, ensuring the enforcement of laws and resolving disputes within the community.

In conclusion, Maya government was characterized by a hierarchical structure, with city-state rulers supported by a council of nobles. Decision-making involved consultation and consensus-building, while religion played a significant role in maintaining political and social order. The decentralized nature of the Maya civilization allowed for the diversity of city-states, while political alliances and conflicts shaped their interactions. The Maya government, with its complex system of governance, was an essential component of their thriving civilization and contributed to their remarkable cultural and intellectual achievements.

Mayan Daily Life

The Maya civilization, known for its remarkable achievements in art, architecture, and astronomy, flourished in Mesoamerica from 2000 BCE to 1500 CE. A closer look at Maya daily life provides a fascinating insight into their culture, social structure, and daily activities.

The Maya society was primarily agrarian, with farming forming the backbone of their economy. Men and women had distinct roles: men were responsible for agricultural activities such as clearing fields, planting, and harvesting crops, while women focused on tasks like cooking, weaving, and raising children. This division of labor reflected the Maya's deep connection with the land and their understanding of the importance of maintaining harmony with nature.

Family was the foundation of Maya society. Extended families lived together in compounds consisting of several houses. These compounds were often organized around a central courtyard and shared common spaces. The Maya practiced matrilineal descent, meaning that family lineage was traced through the mother's side, and inheritance passed from mother to daughter. The elders played a crucial role in decision-making and were highly respected for their wisdom and guidance.

Religion held immense significance in Maya daily life. They believed in a complex pantheon of gods and worshipped them through rituals, ceremonies, and offerings. Temples and pyramids served as sacred spaces for religious practices. The Maya believed that by performing these rituals, they could maintain the cosmic balance and ensure the well-being of their community.

Education was highly valued among the Maya. Young boys and girls received instruction from elders and specialized teachers, who passed down knowledge of history, mathematics, astronomy, and writing. Maya writing was a sophisticated system of hieroglyphs that recorded important events, historical accounts, and religious texts. Skilled scribes played a crucial role in the preservation and dissemination of knowledge.

Art and creativity were integral to Maya daily life. They excelled in pottery, weaving, and the production of intricate jewelry. Murals and sculptures adorned the walls of temples and palaces, depicting scenes from daily life, mythological stories, and religious rituals. These artistic expressions reflected their reverence for beauty, symbolism, and the spiritual realm.

Sports and recreational activities played an important role in Maya society. Ball games, such as the famous Mesoamerican ballgame, were not just entertainment but also had deep cultural and religious significance. These games were often accompanied by rituals and served as a way to honor gods, settle disputes, and maintain social cohesion.

In conclusion, Maya daily life was deeply rooted in their agricultural practices, family structures, religious beliefs, and artistic expressions. The Maya's reverence for nature, strong social ties, and pursuit of knowledge shaped their daily routines and contributed to their remarkable cultural and intellectual achievements. Exploring Maya daily life offers us a glimpse into the rich tapestry of an ancient civilization that thrived centuries ago, leaving behind a legacy that continues to captivate and inspire us today.

Mayan Pyramids & Architecture

The Maya civilization, renowned for its architectural marvels and cultural achievements, left behind a legacy of impressive pyramids and architectural wonders. These structures, with their grandeur and precision, provide valuable insights into the advanced engineering and profound spirituality of the Maya people. Exploring Maya pyramids and architecture takes us on a journey through their rich history and reveals the sophistication of their civilization.

Maya pyramids served as sacred ceremonial centers and were focal points for religious rituals and astronomical observations. These pyramids were not merely physical structures but were believed to be portals connecting the earthly realm with the celestial realm. The Maya viewed the pyramids as representations of sacred mountains, where gods and ancestors resided. Each pyramid was meticulously aligned with celestial events, such as solstices and equinoxes, demonstrating the Maya's deep connection with the cosmos.

The architecture of Maya pyramids was characterized by precise planning and construction techniques. They were built using stone, often limestone, which was cut into large blocks and carefully fitted together. The Maya mastered the art of quarrying, shaping, and transporting these massive stones to create intricate structures that stood the test of time. The pyramids were adorned with elaborate carvings, hieroglyphic inscriptions, and decorative elements that showcased the Maya's artistic prowess.

The most famous Maya pyramid is the Pyramid of Kukulkan at Chichen Itza. This pyramid, also known as El Castillo, is a remarkable example of Maya architectural excellence. It features a series of terraces, staircases, and platforms leading to a temple at the top. The pyramid is precisely designed to create a remarkable visual effect during the equinoxes, where the shadow cast by the setting sun resembles a serpent descending the staircase.

Another notable Maya site is Tikal, where towering pyramids rise above the dense jungle canopy. The Temple of the Great Jaguar and the Temple of the Masks are architectural wonders that showcase the intricacy and grandeur of Maya construction. These pyramids were not only religious structures but also served as monumental tombs for revered rulers and ancestors.

Maya architecture extended beyond pyramids to include other structures such as palaces, ball courts, and observatories. Palaces, with their multiple rooms and courtyards, housed the ruling elite and served as administrative centers. Ball courts were arenas for the famous Maya ballgame, a ritualistic sport with deep religious significance. Observatories, with their precise alignments and astronomical knowledge, were used to study celestial events and further the Maya's understanding of the cosmos.

In conclusion, Maya pyramids and architecture are testament to the remarkable achievements of the ancient Maya civilization. These structures were not only physical representations of religious and ceremonial importance but also showcased the Maya's advanced engineering skills and deep spiritual beliefs. Maya pyramids stand as enduring symbols of a civilization that valued the harmony between the earthly and celestial realms, leaving behind a legacy that continues to captivate and inspire us today.

Mayan Education

Education played a pivotal role in the flourishing Maya civilization, enabling the development of advanced knowledge, skills, and cultural practices. Through a sophisticated system of learning, the Maya imparted valuable expertise in various fields, contributing to their remarkable achievements in astronomy, mathematics, writing, and more.

Structured Learning (93 words): Maya education was highly organized and structured. Young Maya boys and girls attended separate schools where they received specialized instruction. The curriculum focused on diverse subjects, including mathematics, astronomy, writing, history, religion, and art. Skilled teachers, often priests or scribes, imparted knowledge through oral teachings, demonstrations, and practical exercises. Maya students were encouraged to ask questions, engage in discussions, and participate in hands-on learning experiences, fostering a deep understanding of complex concepts.

Mathematics and Astronomy (94 words): The Maya excelled in mathematics and astronomy, developing a sophisticated numerical system and intricate calendar. Students learned advanced mathematical concepts, including arithmetic, geometry, and algebra, which were applied to practical situations such as agriculture and trade. Astronomy held great significance, as the Maya possessed detailed astronomical observations and predictions. Students were taught celestial movements, the cycles of planets, and the concept of time, which formed the basis of their precise calendar system.

Writing and Hieroglyphics (76 words): The Maya had a complex writing system composed of hieroglyphic symbols. Education included instruction in reading, writing, and deciphering these intricate glyphs. Students practiced inscribing on bark paper or stone surfaces to hone their skills. This knowledge allowed the Maya to record historical events, religious ceremonies, astronomical observations, and cultural traditions, preserving their rich heritage for future generations.

Cultural and Practical Education (85 words): Maya education extended beyond academic subjects. Students also received training in practical skills such as agriculture, craftsmanship, and trade. They learned techniques for cultivating crops, crafting intricate pottery, weaving textiles, and creating artistic masterpieces. This holistic approach ensured a well-rounded education that fostered not only intellectual growth but also the development of practical skills crucial for everyday life.

Conclusion (27 words): Education was an integral part of Maya society, shaping their remarkable accomplishments. The sophisticated system of learning enabled the Maya to advance in various fields, leaving a lasting legacy of knowledge and innovation.

Mayan Art

The ancient Maya civilization, known for its advanced achievements in science, architecture, and writing, also left an indelible mark in the realm of art. The intricate and captivating artwork of the Maya people offers us a glimpse into their rich culture and beliefs. From monumental sculptures to delicate pottery, Maya art showcases their creativity, skill, and profound connection with the natural and spiritual worlds.

Maya art flourished throughout the region of Mesoamerica, encompassing present-day Mexico, Guatemala, Belize, Honduras, and El Salvador. It spanned over thousands of years, from the Preclassic period (2000 BCE - 250 CE) to the Postclassic period (900 - 1521 CE). During this time, Maya artists produced a diverse range of artistic expressions, each with its own unique style and symbolism.

One of the most recognizable forms of Maya art is their stone sculptures. These imposing works depicted rulers, gods, and supernatural beings. Maya sculptors skillfully carved intricate details, showcasing elaborate headdresses, jewelry, and garments. These sculptures often adorned the facades of temples and palaces, serving as a visual representation of the ruling elite's power and authority.

The Maya also excelled in the art of pottery. Their ceramics were not only utilitarian but also served as a canvas for intricate designs and narratives. Maya pottery was decorated with vibrant colors and intricate patterns that depicted scenes from everyday life, mythology, and rituals. The delicate brushwork and attention to detail exhibited in their pottery are a testament to the artistic sophistication of the Maya.

Another distinctive feature of Maya art is their intricate hieroglyphic writing system, which combined both phonetic and logographic elements. Maya scribes skillfully carved glyphs onto stone monuments, stucco walls, and codices (screenfold books made of bark paper). These inscriptions provided invaluable insights into Maya history, mythology, and rituals.

The natural world held great significance in Maya art. Animals, plants, and celestial bodies were often depicted, reflecting the Maya's deep spiritual connection with their environment. Jaguars, birds, serpents, and maize were recurrent motifs, symbolizing various deities and aspects of the natural world. The Maya believed that these representations held the power to connect the earthly and divine realms.

Maya art not only served aesthetic purposes but also played a vital role in religious and ceremonial contexts. Murals adorned the walls of sacred spaces, depicting scenes from creation myths and important rituals. Elaborate codices, such as the famous Dresden Codex, contained astronomical and calendrical information, as well as religious ceremonies and prophecies.

While the ancient Maya civilization declined centuries ago, their art continues to captivate and inspire people today. Archaeologists, art historians, and enthusiasts delve into the intricate details and symbolism, unraveling the stories embedded within these masterpieces. Maya art serves as a bridge connecting us to their vibrant world, allowing us to appreciate their creativity, cultural depth, and the enduring legacy of this remarkable civilization.

In conclusion, Maya art stands as a testament to the artistic genius and cultural richness of the ancient Maya civilization. From monumental sculptures to delicate pottery and intricate hieroglyphic inscriptions, their art provides us with a window into their lives, beliefs, and aspirations. Through their masterful creations, the Maya artists conveyed their profound connection with the natural and spiritual realms, leaving behind a legacy that continues to fascinate and inspire us to this day.

Mayan Calendar

The ancient Maya civilization, renowned for their advancements in science, mathematics, and astronomy, developed a complex and sophisticated calendar system. The Maya calendar served as a crucial tool for organizing time, predicting celestial events, and understanding the cyclical nature of life. With its intricate interplay of calendars and astronomical observations, the Maya calendar remains a testament to their intellectual prowess and deep connection with the cosmos.

The Maya calendar system consisted of multiple calendars that worked in harmony to track different aspects of time. The most well-known of these calendars is the Long Count, which measured time in long cycles called baktuns, with each baktun encompassing approximately 394 years. The Long Count calendar provided a linear count of days, allowing the Maya to record historical events and mark significant cosmic occurrences.

In addition to the Long Count, the Maya employed other calendars such as the Haab and the Tzolk'in. The Haab, known as the civil calendar, consisted of 365 days divided into 18 months of 20 days each, with an additional five-day period known as the Wayeb'. The Haab calendar aligned with the solar year and was primarily used for agricultural and civil purposes.

The Tzolk'in, often referred to as the sacred calendar, was a 260-day cycle that played a vital role in religious and ceremonial contexts. Composed of 20 named days combined with 13 numerical coefficients, the Tzolk'in cycled through a unique combination of day names and numbers, creating a repeating pattern that only reset every 260 days. This calendar was believed to govern human destiny and was consulted for divination and timing important events.

The Maya calendar system also incorporated astronomical observations, particularly those related to the movement of celestial bodies. The Maya were adept astronomers who carefully observed the paths of the sun, moon, and planets. They were able to predict astronomical phenomena such as eclipses and the movements of Venus, which held significant religious and symbolic importance in Maya culture.

The Maya calendar not only served practical purposes but also held deep spiritual and cultural significance. It was believed to be a reflection of the cosmic order and a means to commune with the gods. Maya rituals and ceremonies were often timed according to the alignments and cycles of the calendar. The calendar also played a role in the Maya's understanding of creation myths, divine hierarchies, and the cyclical nature of time and life.

Despite the decline of the ancient Maya civilization, their calendar system continues to captivate modern scholars and enthusiasts. Researchers have dedicated extensive efforts to decode and understand the intricate workings of the Maya calendar. The insights gained from the calendar have shed light on the Maya's sophisticated understanding of astronomy, mathematics, and their interconnected worldview.

In conclusion, the Maya calendar stands as a remarkable achievement of the ancient Maya civilization. With its interplay of different calendars, astronomical observations, and spiritual significance, the Maya calendar system exemplifies their intellectual prowess and deep connection with the cosmos. Today, the Maya calendar serves as a testament to their enduring legacy, reminding us of the intricate and awe-inspiring nature of their civilization.

Mayan Codex

The Maya Codex is a fascinating artifact that provides valuable insights into the ancient Maya civilization. Codices were books made of bark paper or deerskin and served as repositories of knowledge, containing important historical, astronomical, and religious information. These codices were an integral part of Maya culture, documenting their complex society and their deep connection with the natural world.

The Maya Codex is a testament to the advanced intellectual and scientific achievements of the Maya people. It contains intricate hieroglyphic writing, vibrant illustrations, and numerical calculations that depict their understanding of astronomy, mathematics, and the passage of time. These codices were highly revered and meticulously crafted by Maya scribes, who were well-versed in the complex writing system.

One of the most well-known Maya codices is the Dresden Codex, named after the city in Germany where it is housed. It is a long, accordion-style book that measures nearly three meters in length when unfolded. The Dresden Codex focuses on astronomy and contains detailed astronomical tables, predictions of celestial events, and information on the Venus cycle.

Another notable Maya codex is the Madrid Codex, which offers valuable insights into Maya religious beliefs and rituals. It features illustrations of gods and ceremonial scenes, as well as information on the calendar system and divination practices. The Madrid Codex is an essential resource for understanding Maya cosmology and their deep spiritual connection with the supernatural world.

Unfortunately, many Maya codices were destroyed during the Spanish conquest of the Americas in the 16th century. The Spanish colonizers considered them pagan artifacts and sought to eradicate Maya culture. However, a few codices survived, providing a glimpse into the rich cultural heritage of the Maya civilization.

The study of the Maya Codex has greatly contributed to our understanding of ancient Maya society. It has helped decipher their complex hieroglyphic writing system, enabling scholars to translate and interpret other Maya inscriptions found on stelae, pottery, and architectural structures. The codices have shed light on Maya political organization, religious practices, agricultural techniques, and their sophisticated understanding of the natural world.

Today, the surviving Maya codices are carefully preserved and studied by archaeologists, anthropologists, and linguists. Digital technology has played a crucial role in preserving these fragile artifacts and making them accessible to a wider audience. With ongoing research and advancements in deciphering the Maya script, we continue to uncover the secrets held within the pages of these ancient codices.

In conclusion, the Maya Codex serves as a significant link to the ancient Maya civilization, providing us with valuable knowledge about their history, culture, and intellectual achievements. These remarkable artifacts are a testament to the Maya's profound understanding of astronomy, mathematics, and their complex religious beliefs. The surviving codices are not only treasures of the past but also a source of inspiration and wonder for future generations, highlighting the richness and diversity of human civilization throughout history.

Mayan Food

Maya cuisine offers a captivating glimpse into the culinary traditions of the ancient Maya civilization, which flourished in Mesoamerica from 2000 BCE to 1500 CE. A closer look at Maya food reveals not only their dietary practices but also their cultural values and deep connection with the natural world.

The Maya people were skilled farmers, and their agricultural practices formed the foundation of their food culture. Corn, also known as maize, was the staple crop and the centerpiece of Maya meals. They cultivated various varieties of corn and used it as a base for a multitude of dishes. Corn was often ground into flour to make tortillas, tamales, and various types of bread.

Beans and squash were important complementary crops in the Maya diet. Beans provided a rich source of protein, while squash added nutritional diversity. These three crops, known as the "Three Sisters," were often grown together in a sustainable agricultural practice known as companion planting.

The Maya also incorporated a wide variety of vegetables and fruits into their meals. Avocado, tomatoes, peppers, and various leafy greens were commonly used ingredients. Fruits such as papaya, pineapple, and guava added a touch of sweetness to their cuisine.

Meat, particularly wild game, played a significant role in Maya food. They hunted animals such as deer, rabbit, and turkey, and also fished in rivers and coastal areas. These sources of protein were often cooked with aromatic herbs and spices to create flavorful stews and roasted dishes.

The Maya had a deep appreciation for the flavors of their food and used a range of herbs, spices, and condiments to enhance their dishes. Achiote, a bright red spice derived from the seeds of the annatto tree, was a staple in Maya cooking, adding both color and flavor. Other common seasonings included cilantro, cacao, and chili peppers, which added heat and complexity to their meals.

Food was not merely sustenance for the Maya but also a way to express their cultural values and beliefs. Ritual feasting played an important role in Maya society, where food was prepared and consumed as offerings to the gods or as part of religious ceremonies. These feasts were occasions for communal gatherings and celebrations, reinforcing social bonds and expressing gratitude.

Today, Maya cuisine continues to be celebrated and preserved by their descendants. Traditional cooking techniques and recipes have been passed down through generations, keeping the culinary traditions alive. Maya dishes can still be savored, showcasing the rich and diverse flavors that reflect the ancient heritage of this fascinating civilization.

In conclusion, Maya food is an integral part of their cultural identity, reflecting their agricultural practices, culinary skills, and spiritual beliefs. The reliance on corn, the use of native ingredients, and the artful combination of flavors are testaments to their deep connection with the natural world. Exploring Maya food not only offers a taste of their ancient cuisine but also provides insight into the rich tapestry of their traditions, sustenance, and cultural heritage.

Mayan Gods & Mythology

The Maya civilization, renowned for its sophisticated art, architecture, and astronomical knowledge, held a deep spiritual connection with a rich pantheon of gods. Their mythology, a tapestry of captivating stories and beliefs, provides a fascinating insight into the Maya's spiritual worldview.

The Maya gods represented various aspects of nature, celestial bodies, and human experiences. They embodied both benevolent and malevolent forces and were believed to have power over the natural world and human affairs. Each god had unique characteristics, symbols, and roles in the Maya cosmology.

Among the prominent deities was Itzamna, the supreme god and ruler of the heavens. Itzamna was associated with creation, wisdom, and the sacred calendar. Another significant figure was Chaac, the god of rain and fertility. The Maya relied on Chaac's benevolence to ensure bountiful harvests and agricultural prosperity.

The mythology also included gods such as Kukulkan, the feathered serpent deity associated with wisdom and resurrection, and Ixchel, the goddess of fertility, childbirth, and the moon. Ixchel played a vital role in the cycle of life and was invoked by women seeking assistance in matters of reproduction and motherhood.

Mythical stories were woven into the fabric of Maya society, passed down through generations in oral traditions. These stories explained the origins of the world, the purpose of humanity, and the interplay between gods and mortals. They reflected the Maya's profound reverence for the natural world and their place within it.

Maya mythology was closely intertwined with astronomical observations. The movements of celestial bodies, such as the sun, moon, and Venus, were believed to influence human destinies and determine auspicious times for rituals and ceremonies. Maya priests, known as ah kinob, were responsible for interpreting these celestial events and guiding the people in their spiritual practices.

The Maya performed elaborate rituals and ceremonies to honor their gods. Temples and pyramids served as sacred spaces where offerings were made, including food, flowers, and precious objects. Bloodletting rituals, in which individuals would pierce their skin to offer their blood, were practiced as a symbol of devotion and to establish a spiritual connection with the gods.

While many aspects of Maya mythology remain enigmatic, ongoing research and archaeological discoveries continue to shed light on their complex belief system. The decipherment of Maya hieroglyphic writing has revealed inscriptions and narratives that provide deeper insights into their gods and mythological traditions.

In conclusion, Maya gods and mythology were integral to their spiritual and cultural identity. The belief in a pantheon of gods and the rich tapestry of mythological stories reflected their deep reverence for nature, their understanding of the celestial realm, and their place within the cosmos. Exploring Maya gods and mythology offers a captivating journey into an ancient civilization's worldview and their quest to understand the mysteries of existence.

Chaac

The Maya civilization, renowned for its complex cosmology and remarkable achievements, held great reverence for nature and its deities. Among their pantheon of gods, Chaac stood out as the powerful deity responsible for rain, thunder, and lightning—a vital force in sustaining life in the ancient Maya world.

Chaac played a central role in Maya society as the god of rain and agriculture. The Maya, primarily an agricultural community, depended on Chaac's benevolence to ensure bountiful harvests. As the deity responsible for rain, Chaac was believed to control the seasonal cycles and bring the much-needed rainfall for crops to thrive. The Maya worshipped Chaac through rituals and offerings, seeking his favor for agricultural prosperity. The importance of Chaac's role extended beyond agriculture, as rain was also seen as a symbol of life and fertility, essential for the well-being and sustenance of the entire community.

Chaac was often depicted as a man with reptilian features, including a serpent-like nose and fangs. He was portrayed holding a stone axe, known as a "lightning axe," representing his control over thunder and lightning. The Maya associated these natural phenomena with Chaac's presence. Chaac's association with water and rain was further emphasized through his headdress, which featured large curved objects resembling serpent fangs. The serpent was a symbol of water and life in Maya cosmology, highlighting the profound connection between Chaac and the life-sustaining force of rain.

To honor Chaac, the Maya conducted elaborate rituals and ceremonies, often held at sacred cenotes or natural wells. These rituals involved offerings of food, drink, and other valuable items. In some instances, the Maya performed bloodletting rituals as a way to please Chaac and ensure rainfall. The belief was that blood offerings would nourish and invigorate the deity, encouraging him to bring forth rain for the benefit of the people. These ceremonies served as a vital link between the Maya community and the divine, reinforcing their spiritual connection with the powerful and unpredictable forces of nature.

Chaac, the mighty rain god of the Maya, held a significant position in their religious and agricultural practices. The Maya's reliance on Chaac's benevolence for their sustenance underscores the vital role that nature and its deities played in their lives, shaping their culture and worldview.

Itzamná

Itzamná, the supreme deity of the Maya civilization, held a significant place in their complex religious beliefs. Revered as the creator of the world and the patron of knowledge and wisdom, Itzamná played a central role in Maya mythology, rituals, and societal norms. Exploring the characteristics and importance of Itzamná provides insight into the rich spiritual and cultural heritage of the Maya people.

According to Maya mythology, Itzamná was born from the primordial sea and emerged as a divine being with vast knowledge and power. Often depicted as an elderly figure with a long white beard, Itzamná embodied wisdom, learning, and the celestial realm. The deity was associated with the sun, moon, and stars, representing the interconnectedness of the natural world and the divine. Itzamná was also believed to possess the ability to communicate with humans, guiding them in matters of agriculture, medicine, and religious ceremonies.

Itzamná held a crucial place in Maya religious practices. Temples and altars dedicated to Itzamná were constructed throughout Maya cities, and the deity was worshipped through rituals and offerings. The Maya believed that Itzamná played a vital role in maintaining the balance of the universe and ensuring the prosperity of their society. Itzamná's guidance was sought in matters of governance, agriculture, and healing, as well as in celestial events and the calendar system.

Itzamná's influence extended beyond religious beliefs. The deity's association with knowledge and wisdom made Itzamná a symbol of intellectual pursuits, education, and cultural development. Itzamná's presence can be seen in Maya art, architecture, and literature, reflecting the reverence and respect given to this supreme deity. The enduring legacy of Itzamná serves as a reminder of the Maya civilization's deep spiritual beliefs, intellectual achievements, and intricate understanding of the natural world.

Kukulkan

In the rich mythology of the ancient Maya civilization, one deity stands out as a symbol of power, wisdom, and transformation. Kukulkan, often depicted as a magnificent, feathered serpent, captivated the hearts and minds of the Maya people. With its fascinating legends and awe-inspiring temples, Kukulkan remains an enigma, evoking curiosity and wonder to this day.

Kukulkan, also known as Quetzalcoatl to the Aztecs, was a prominent god worshipped throughout Mesoamerica. The name "Kukulkan" is derived from the Maya words "k'uk'ul" (feather) and "kan" (snake), emphasizing the divine serpent's association with both the earth and the sky. This dual nature reflects the Maya belief in the interconnectedness of all things.

According to legend, Kukulkan descended from the heavens to bring knowledge and civilization to the Maya people. It is said that he taught them agriculture, astronomy, and the arts, enlightening their society and establishing harmony. This benevolent deity was considered the protector of rulers and was often associated with fertility and rain, crucial elements for the Maya's agricultural-based civilization.

One of the most remarkable manifestations of Kukulkan's influence can be seen in the architectural marvels of the Maya city of Chichen Itza. The grand pyramid known as El Castillo, or the Temple of Kukulkan, is a testament to the reverence the Maya held for this deity. This step pyramid, standing tall at over 30 meters, is an astonishing sight. Its unique design showcases Kukulkan's symbolism with four staircases, each with 91 steps, adding up to 365 steps in total, representing the solar year.

One of the most breathtaking aspects of El Castillo occurs during the spring and autumn equinoxes. As the sun sets, a shadowy serpent appears to descend the pyramid's staircase. This phenomenon, known as the "Descent of Kukulkan," is a testament to the Maya's deep astronomical knowledge and their reverence for the cycles of the natural world.

Beyond Chichen Itza, Kukulkan's presence can be found in numerous Maya city-states across the Yucatan Peninsula. Artistic representations depict him as a feathered serpent, adorned with vibrant plumage and intricate scales. These images not only capture the imagination but also serve as a reminder of the Maya's deep spiritual connection with the natural world.

Although the Maya civilization experienced a decline in the 10th century CE, the legacy of Kukulkan endures. The mysterious feathered serpent continues to fascinate scholars, archaeologists, and tourists alike, drawing them to the ancient ruins in search of a deeper understanding of this remarkable deity.

Kukulkan's influence extends beyond the boundaries of time and space, transcending cultural barriers. Today, the feathered serpent remains an emblem of wisdom, transformation, and the eternal cycles of life. Whether it be through the stories told by the Maya, the awe-inspiring architecture of their temples, or the modern-day explorations of researchers, Kukulkan continues to be a symbol of wonder and inspiration, reminding us of the enduring power of mythology and the profound connection between humans and the natural world.

Hero Twins Myth

Long ago, in the heart of the ancient Mayan civilization, there lived a pair of extraordinary twins named Hunahpu and Xbalanque. These brothers were no ordinary boys; they were destined for greatness, chosen by the gods to embark on a heroic journey that would test their courage, wit, and strength.

Hunahpu and Xbalanque were born to a humble family, yet from an early age, it was clear that they possessed remarkable talents. They excelled in hunting, fishing, and various other skills, earning the admiration of their peers and the respect of their elders.

But their peaceful existence was soon disrupted by the wicked lords of the underworld, known as the Lords of Xibalba. These malevolent beings ruled over the dark realm beneath the earth, spreading fear and misery among the living. Determined to rid the world of their evil influence, the Hero Twins embarked on a perilous quest to confront the Lords of Xibalba and restore balance to the world.

Armed with bravery and cunning, Hunahpu and Xbalanque journeyed deep into the heart of the underworld, facing numerous challenges and obstacles along the way. They encountered treacherous rivers, impassable mountains, and fierce beasts, yet they remained undaunted in their quest.

As they ventured deeper into the realm of Xibalba, the Hero Twins encountered the first of the Lords, who sought to test their strength and resilience. They were subjected to trials of endurance and skill, forced to overcome obstacles that tested their courage and determination.

Despite the Lords' best efforts to thwart them, Hunahpu and Xbalanque proved themselves to be resourceful and clever. They outwitted their adversaries with cunning traps and clever ruses, gradually gaining the upper hand in their quest.

Along the way, the Hero Twins received aid and guidance from various allies, including the wise owl and the cunning spider. These loyal companions provided valuable advice and assistance, helping them navigate the dangers of the underworld and stay one step ahead of their foes.

Finally, after many trials and tribulations, Hunahpu and Xbalanque reached the throne room of the Lords of Xibalba. There, they faced the ultimate challenge: a deadly ballgame that would determine the fate of the world.

The ballgame was no ordinary contest; it was a test of skill, strength, and strategy, with the stakes higher than ever before. The Hero Twins squared off against the Lords of Xibalba in a fierce competition, each side vying for victory and control of the earth.

Despite the Lords' best efforts to cheat and deceive, Hunahpu and Xbalanque remained steadfast and focused. With skillful plays and clever maneuvers, they emerged victorious, defeating the Lords of Xibalba and banishing them from the world forever.

In the aftermath of their triumph, peace and prosperity were restored to the land, thanks to the bravery and sacrifice of the Hero Twins. Their heroic deeds became the stuff of legend, celebrated in stories and songs throughout the Mayan civilization.

And so, the tale of the Hero Twins endures as a testament to the power of courage, determination, and brotherly love. Hunahpu and Xbalanque may have been born as humble boys, but through their courage and sacrifice, they became true heroes, forever remembered and revered in the annals of Mayan history.

Mayan Warfare

The Maya civilization, known for its cultural achievements and architectural wonders, also had a complex system of warfare. Maya warfare played a significant role in their society, shaping political alliances, territorial expansion, and social hierarchy. Exploring Maya warfare provides us with valuable insights into their military strategies and the dynamics of this ancient civilization.

Maya warfare was primarily driven by competition for resources, territory, and political power. The Maya city-states engaged in conflicts and battles to protect their interests and assert their dominance. Warfare was not only a means of securing resources but also a way to demonstrate bravery, honor, and prowess in battle.

The Maya warriors were highly trained and disciplined. They underwent rigorous military training from a young age, honing their skills in combat, archery, and tactics. Maya warriors were skilled in using various weapons, including obsidian-bladed swords, spears, and atlatls (spear-throwing devices). They also wore protective armor made from materials such as wood, bone, and animal hides.

Maya warfare strategies involved both offensive and defensive tactics. Cities were fortified with defensive walls, watchtowers, and moats to protect against enemy attacks. Military campaigns often involved surprise assaults, ambushes, and sieges. Maya warriors used guerrilla tactics, striking swiftly and withdrawing into the jungles, making it difficult for their enemies to pursue them.

Warfare in the Maya civilization was not limited to physical confrontations. Psychological warfare played a significant role as well. Intimidation tactics, such as displaying captured enemies or performing ritualistic sacrifices, aimed to instill fear and weaken the morale of opposing forces. Maya rulers and warriors were also renowned for their propaganda campaigns, using art, sculptures, and inscriptions to glorify military victories and convey their power.

The Maya had a complex system of military organization. Each city-state had its own standing army, commanded by a military leader known as a batab. These leaders formed alliances and coalitions with neighboring city-states to strengthen their military forces and engage in large-scale conflicts. Maya warfare was also intertwined with religious beliefs, with gods of war and death playing important roles in battles and military rituals.

The end of a battle or war was often marked by the capture of prisoners. Prisoners of war were either sacrificed in elaborate rituals to please the gods or used as laborers or slaves. The capture of prisoners held immense cultural and political significance, serving as a display of power and dominance.

In conclusion, Maya warfare was a complex and integral part of the ancient Maya civilization. The Maya employed advanced military strategies, honed their skills through rigorous training, and utilized psychological warfare to secure their interests and assert their dominance. Maya warfare reflects the complexities of their society, where political power, resources, and religious beliefs intersected. Exploring Maya warfare provides us with a deeper understanding of this remarkable civilization and its contributions to history.

Tikal-Calakmul War

The Tikal-Calakmul Wars, a protracted and impactful conflict that unfolded within the ancient Maya civilization, marked a significant chapter in Mesoamerican history. This rivalry between two powerful city-states, Tikal and Calakmul, played out over centuries and had profound implications for the political dynamics of the Maya region during the Classic period (250 CE to 900 CE).

At the heart of the conflict was the struggle for supremacy and dominance between Tikal, located in the lowland rainforests of present-day Guatemala, and Calakmul, situated in the heart of the Yucatán Peninsula. Both cities were flourishing centers of Mayan civilization, characterized by grand architecture, intricate hieroglyphic inscriptions, and complex political structures.

Calakmul, under the leadership of the Snake Kings, a lineage of powerful rulers associated with serpent iconography, sought to extend its influence and control over the broader Maya region. The Snake Kings wielded significant political power within Calakmul and aspired to shape the political and cultural landscape on a larger scale.

Tikal, on the other hand, was an equally influential city-state with its own ambitions for regional dominance. As these two powerful entities vied for control, the Tikal-Calakmul Wars became a defining feature of Maya geopolitics. The conflict involved military campaigns, strategic alliances, and shifting allegiances, creating a complex web of political maneuvers and engagements.

The Tikal-Calakmul Wars were not merely isolated military clashes but a series of interconnected events that unfolded over an extended period. These wars were characterized by periods of intense conflict, where Tikal and Calakmul engaged in military confrontations, and periods of relative peace, marked by strategic alliances and diplomatic efforts.

One of the key battlegrounds in this conflict was the expansive and diverse Maya lowlands. Cities and smaller polities aligned themselves with either Tikal or Calakmul, drawn into the broader struggle for supremacy. The outcome of individual battles and campaigns had a cascading effect on the overall balance of power within the Maya region.

The rulers of Tikal and Calakmul, each driven by a desire to secure their city-state's dominance, engaged in a dynamic interplay of military strategy and political maneuvering. Calakmul's Snake Kings, with their powerful political lineage and advanced understanding of Maya hieroglyphic writing, left an enduring mark on the conflict's historical record through inscriptions and monuments.

The Tikal-Calakmul Wars also had a profound impact on the architectural landscape of both cities. The need to fortify against external threats and demonstrate political authority led to the construction of impressive defensive structures, including walls and watchtowers. Additionally, the rulers commissioned grand monuments, such as stelae and pyramids, to commemorate military victories and reinforce their divine connections.

The protracted nature of the Tikal-Calakmul Wars underscores the complexity of Maya geopolitics during the Classic period. The conflicts and alliances forged during this time laid the groundwork for the ever-shifting political landscape of the Maya region, contributing to the intricate tapestry of Mesoamerican history. Despite the intensity of the rivalry, both Tikal and Calakmul experienced periods of ascendancy

Mayan Writing & Numbers

The Maya civilization, known for its remarkable achievements in art, architecture, and astronomy, also possessed a sophisticated system of writing and numbers. The Maya script, a complex combination of glyphs and symbols, allowed them to record their history, religious beliefs, and astronomical knowledge. The Maya numerical system, based on a vigesimal or base-20 system, enabled them to perform advanced calculations and accurately record quantities. Exploring Maya writing and numbers provides us with a glimpse into the intellectual prowess of this ancient civilization.

The Maya writing system is one of the few fully developed writing systems in the pre-Columbian Americas. It combines pictographic elements with logograms, which represent words or ideas. The Maya script consists of hundreds of different glyphs, each with its own meaning or sound. These glyphs were combined to create intricate compositions that conveyed complex messages.

The Maya script was primarily used for recording historical events, religious rituals, and genealogies. It was also employed in the creation of elaborate inscriptions on temples, monuments, and stelae. Maya scribes, highly trained individuals, dedicated their lives to the art of writing and were responsible for preserving and transmitting knowledge through their meticulously crafted texts.

The Maya numerical system, based on a vigesimal system, used a combination of dots and bars to represent quantities. The dot represented the value of one, while a bar represented the value of five. By combining these symbols, the Maya were able to represent numbers up to nineteen. To represent higher numbers, they employed a place-value system, similar to our decimal system, where the value of a symbol depended on its position.

The Maya numerical system allowed for advanced calculations, including addition, subtraction, multiplication, and division. It also facilitated precise astronomical observations, enabling them to predict celestial events with remarkable accuracy. The Maya had a deep understanding of mathematical concepts, which they applied in various fields, such as architecture, calendar systems, and agricultural practices.

For many years, Maya writing remained a mystery to scholars. It was not until the mid-20th century that significant progress was made in deciphering the Maya script. Through the efforts of dedicated researchers and breakthroughs in comparative linguistics, key advancements were made in understanding the structure and meaning of Maya glyphs.

Today, much progress has been made in deciphering Maya writing, allowing us to gain insights into Maya history, culture, and mythology. The decipherment of Maya inscriptions has shed light on the accomplishments of individual rulers, their military campaigns, and religious ceremonies. It has also provided valuable information about Maya societal structure, trade networks, and intellectual pursuits.

In conclusion, Maya writing and numbers represent a remarkable achievement of the ancient Maya civilization. The intricate Maya script allowed for the recording and preservation of knowledge, while their advanced numerical system enabled sophisticated calculations and precise astronomical observations. The decipherment of Maya writing has expanded our understanding of this ancient civilization and continues to uncover new discoveries, deepening our appreciation for their intellectual and cultural contributions.

Mayan Women

The role of women in the Maya civilization was diverse and multifaceted, reflecting the complexities of their society. While Maya society was predominantly patriarchal, women held significant positions and made invaluable contributions to their community, culture, and economy. Exploring the role of women in the Maya civilization provides us with a deeper understanding of their social structure and gender dynamics.

In Maya society, women played essential roles within the family unit. They were responsible for the upbringing and education of children, passing down cultural traditions, and ensuring the well-being of the household. Women were highly respected as mothers and caretakers, and their nurturing qualities were greatly valued.

Beyond their domestic duties, women in the Maya civilization were engaged in various occupations and vocations. They participated in agriculture, weaving, pottery-making, and trade. Women were skilled farmers, cultivating crops such as maize, beans, and squash, which formed the staple diet of the Maya. They also played a crucial role in the production of textiles, creating intricate designs and patterns through their weaving skills. Some women were involved in the production of ceramics, creating beautiful pottery that served both functional and ceremonial purposes.

Women in the Maya civilization also had opportunities to participate in religious and political spheres. Although men predominantly held positions of political power, women of noble birth could attain high-ranking roles as queens or priestesses. They played important roles in religious ceremonies and rituals, serving as intermediaries between the human and divine realms.

Archaeological evidence suggests that some women were buried with elaborate grave goods, indicating their elevated status within the society. These burials suggest that women could hold positions of prestige and influence.

Despite the opportunities available to women, Maya society had its share of gender inequalities. Men typically held more power and authority, especially in matters of governance and warfare. Nevertheless, women were still able to exert influence within their social circles and contribute to the overall functioning of Maya society.

In conclusion, women in the Maya civilization played vital roles in various aspects of life. They were the backbone of the family unit, engaged in agriculture, craft production, trade, and religious activities. While Maya society was predominantly patriarchal, women had opportunities to attain positions of influence and were highly respected for their contributions. The role of women in the Maya civilization reflects the complexities and diversity of a society that recognized and valued their significant contributions.

The Snake Kings

The Mayan Snake Kings, a fascinating and enigmatic aspect of ancient Maya civilization, emerge from the pages of history as powerful rulers who left an indelible mark on the political landscape of Mesoamerica. Flourishing during the Classic period (250 CE to 900 CE), the Snake Kings were a lineage of Maya rulers associated with the prominent city of Calakmul, located in the heart of the Yucatán Peninsula.

At the pinnacle of their influence, the Snake Kings wielded significant political power, and their impact reverberated throughout the Maya world. The title "Snake Kings" is derived from the prominent depiction of serpent iconography associated with these rulers, emphasizing their divine connections and authority. The snake, a potent symbol in Maya cosmology, represented both earthly and supernatural realms, linking the rulers to the divine forces believed to govern the universe.

Calakmul, the primary seat of the Snake Kings, was a formidable city-state engaged in a longstanding rivalry with the equally influential city of Tikal. This rivalry, known as the Tikal-Calakmul Wars, spanned centuries and had profound implications for the political dynamics of the entire Maya region. The Snake Kings played a central role in these conflicts, leading military campaigns and forging alliances to assert their dominance.

The Snake Kings' penchant for monumental architecture is evident in the grand structures they commissioned, including towering pyramids, palaces, and elaborate stelae. These structures served not only as expressions of political power but also as platforms for ritualistic ceremonies that reinforced the rulers' divine connections. The city of Calakmul itself boasted impressive urban planning, reflecting the Snake Kings' commitment to creating a monumental cityscape befitting their prestigious lineage.

The intricate hieroglyphic inscriptions found on stelae and monuments at Calakmul provide crucial insights into the Snake Kings' genealogy, achievements, and political strategies. These inscriptions serve as a testament to the advanced Maya writing system, allowing modern scholars to unravel the complex history of the Snake Kings and their contributions to Maya civilization.

The Snake Kings were not confined to Calakmul, as their influence extended to other city-states within the Maya region. Through strategic alliances and marriage alliances, they created a network of power that transcended individual city boundaries. The Snake Kings' ability to navigate the complex web of Maya politics contributed to the longevity of their dynasty and solidified their status as paramount rulers.

Despite their political prowess, the Snake Kings faced challenges and periods of decline, mirroring the broader cycles of power and influence within the Maya civilization. Environmental factors, warfare, and shifting alliances all played roles in the waxing and waning of the Snake Kings' dominance. The decline of Calakmul marked the end of an era, but the legacy of the Snake Kings persisted in the annals of Maya history.

In conclusion, the Mayan Snake Kings stand as compelling figures in the rich tapestry of ancient Maya civilization. Their political acumen, cultural contributions, and enduring legacy underscore the complexity and sophistication of Maya society. The Snake Kings' story, woven into the narratives of Calakmul and the Tikal-Calakmul Wars, adds a captivating chapter to our understanding of Mesoamerican history, leaving an eternal imprint on the landscape of the ancient Maya world.

Decline of the Mayans

The decline of the Mayan civilization remains one of history's enduring mysteries, with scholars debating the various factors that contributed to its eventual collapse. At its height, the Mayan civilization thrived in the dense jungles of Mesoamerica, building remarkable cities, developing advanced agricultural techniques, and making significant contributions to art, architecture, and astronomy. However, by the end of the 9th century AD, many of these once-great cities lay abandoned, their populations dispersed, and their monumental structures reclaimed by the encroaching jungle.

One of the key factors believed to have played a role in the decline of the Mayan civilization was environmental degradation. The Mayans were skilled farmers who practiced intensive agriculture, utilizing techniques such as slash-and-burn farming and terracing to cultivate crops in the nutrient-poor soils of the region. However, over time, these practices led to deforestation, soil erosion, and depletion of natural resources, which ultimately undermined the sustainability of Mayan society. As the population grew and resources became scarce, food shortages, famine, and social unrest likely ensued, contributing to the collapse of centralized authority and the fragmentation of Mayan city-states.

Another contributing factor to the decline of the Mayan civilization was political instability and internal conflict. Mayan society was organized into independent city-states, each governed by a divine king and competing for power and resources. Over time, rivalries and conflicts between city-states escalated, leading to warfare, conquest, and the eventual collapse of regional alliances. This internal strife weakened the social fabric of Mayan society, eroding trust in political institutions and undermining the stability of centralized authority.

The arrival of foreign invaders, such as the Toltecs and later the Spanish conquistadors, also hastened the decline of the

Mayan civilization. The Toltecs, a powerful civilization from central Mexico, conquered many of the Mayan city-states in the 10th century AD, imposing their own political and cultural influence on the region. Although the Toltec influence waned in subsequent centuries, the arrival of Spanish conquistadors in the 16th century dealt a final blow to the remnants of Mayan civilization. The Spanish conquest brought disease, warfare, forced labor, and colonization, decimating indigenous populations and eradicating traditional Mayan ways of life.

Despite these external pressures and internal challenges, the Mayan civilization did not vanish entirely. Descendants of the ancient Mayans continue to inhabit the region today, preserving their cultural heritage and maintaining connections to their ancestral past. The ruins of ancient Mayan cities, such as Chichen Itza, Tikal, and Palenque, stand as silent witnesses to the achievements and legacy of one of the world's great civilizations.

In conclusion, the decline of the Mayan civilization was a complex and multifaceted process, influenced by a combination of environmental, political, social, and economic factors. Environmental degradation, political instability, internal conflict, and external pressures all contributed to the collapse of Mayan society, leading to the abandonment of once-great cities and the dispersal of populations. Despite its eventual decline, the legacy of the Mayan civilization endures as a testament to the ingenuity, creativity, and resilience of one of the world's most fascinating cultures.

Legacy of the Mayan Civilization

The legacy of the ancient Mayan civilization endures as a testament to their remarkable achievements in art, architecture, astronomy, mathematics, and culture. Despite the decline of their civilization, the Mayans left behind a rich and enduring legacy that continues to captivate and inspire people around the world.

One of the most enduring legacies of the Mayan civilization is their remarkable architectural achievements. The Mayans built impressive cities, temples, pyramids, and palaces, many of which still stand today as testaments to their advanced engineering skills and ingenuity. Architectural wonders such as the towering pyramids of Chichen Itza, the majestic temples of Tikal, and the intricately carved stelae of Copan are a testament to the Mayans' mastery of construction and design.

In addition to their architectural prowess, the Mayans made significant contributions to the fields of astronomy and mathematics. Mayan astronomers developed sophisticated calendrical systems that accurately tracked celestial movements, allowing them to predict eclipses, solstices, and other astronomical events with remarkable precision. The Mayan calendar, with its complex interlocking cycles, remains one of their most enduring legacies and continues to fascinate scholars and enthusiasts alike.

The Mayans also made important contributions to mathematics, developing a sophisticated numerical system based on a combination of dots and bars. This system allowed them to perform complex calculations, including multiplication, division, and advanced astronomical calculations. The Mayans were among the first civilizations in the world to develop the concept of zero, a revolutionary mathematical concept that would later spread to other cultures and pave the way for modern mathematics.

The artistic legacy of the Mayan civilization is also evident in their intricate pottery, sculpture, and textiles. Mayan artisans created stunning works of art depicting gods, kings, and mythical creatures, often adorned with elaborate designs and intricate patterns. These artistic masterpieces provide valuable insights into Mayan religious beliefs, social customs, and daily life, allowing us to better understand and appreciate their rich cultural heritage.

Religion played a central role in Mayan society, and their religious beliefs and rituals left a lasting impact on their culture and legacy. The Mayans worshipped a pantheon of gods and goddesses associated with natural elements, celestial bodies, and societal roles, and their religious rituals often involved elaborate ceremonies, sacrifices, and offerings. The legacy of Mayan religion is evident in the numerous temples, altars, and sacred sites scattered throughout the Mayan heartland, each serving as a testament to their deep spiritual beliefs and practices.

Despite the decline of their civilization, the legacy of the ancient Mayans continues to thrive in the modern world. Descendants of the ancient Mayans still inhabit the regions of Mexico, Guatemala, Belize, Honduras, and El Salvador, preserving their cultural heritage and maintaining connections to their ancestral past. Traditional Mayan customs, languages, and ceremonies are still practiced today, keeping alive the rich traditions and cultural legacy of their ancestors.

The archaeological sites of the ancient Mayan cities, such as Chichen Itza, Tikal, and Palenque, continue to attract millions of visitors from around the world each year, offering a glimpse into the magnificent achievements of this remarkable civilization. These ancient ruins serve as a reminder of the ingenuity, creativity, and resilience of the Mayan people, inspiring awe and wonder in all who visit them.

In conclusion, the legacy of the ancient Mayan civilization is a testament to their remarkable achievements in art, architecture, astronomy, mathematics, and culture. Despite the passage of time, the legacy of the Mayans continues to thrive, inspiring fascination and admiration in people around the world and serving as a lasting tribute to one of the world's great civilizations.